THIS BOOK BELONGS TO:

____

This book is dedicated to my daughter Alice Coleman
And my mother Alice Coleman.

It is also dedicated to all the people in my own Personal Memoir, including Ken Johnson, Dana Johnson, Mike Egan, Ken Medlock, Shecky Mulligan, George Tapps, Tom O'Reilly, Dean Barkley, Alan Krieger, Jack Scalia, Nick Mariano, Lillian Muller, Mary Alice Coleman Dybsky, Ann Coleman Campbell, Tom Coleman, Pat Coleman, Margaret Coleman Gaident, Steve Gadient, Nick Hardin, John Moore, Kristen Hicks, Terry Johnson, Kirby Kitchener, and Carl Triola.

Balboa Press books may be ordered through booksellers or by contacting:
Balboa Press
A Division of Hay House
1663 Liberty Drive
Bloomington, IN 47403
www.balboapress.com
1-(877) 407-4847

ISBN: 978-1-4525-5916-2 (sc)
ISBN: 978-1-4525-5917-9 (e)

Library of Congress Control Number: 2012917767

For additional books contact
John Coleman
310-477-5052
11621 Ayres Ave.
Los Angeles, CA 90064
johnecoleman@verizon.net

Printed in the United States of America

Balboa Press rev. date: 11/19/2012

Who Are You

TREASURED MEMORIES
TREASURED MEMORIES
TREASURED MEMORIES
TREASURED MEMORIES
TREASURED MEMORIES
TREASURED MEMORIES

JOHN E. COLEMAN

Table of Contents

WHO ARE YOU
TREASURED MEMORIES
A Personal Memoir

Just who are you? An interesting question.

We are all a conglomeration of our hopes and dreams, wishes and fears, accomplishments and failures - an amalgam of all the different: 1) experiences we've had, 2) ideas we thought, 3) feelings we felt, and 4) our physical bodies.

Memories are something special and beautiful to be enjoyed and appreciated over and over many times.

Outside of one's family and friends, the greatest things in a person's life are his memories. It's sad that people don't take time to enjoy our memories more often and learn from them and appreciate what we have.

This book allows you to collect your most treasured memories and have an incredible life experience writing them down and recalling them.

Memories are something you can share with your loved ones; memories of your hopes and dreams, memories of your fears, victories and defeats. Some are funny, some are touching, some were painful and some still are. They all are you. When completed, this book can be kept next to the family photo album.

The treasure of memories can be enjoyed again and again.

Some people think it is a self-help book – and it is. But that is not my main intent.

I do know it is a fascinating voyage of self-discovery for all of you.

And I hope the memories in this book will help you remember and appreciate your "Wonderful Life".

DIRECTIONS

Filling in your treasured memories will be both fun and challenging. It should be a joyful endeavor. You will be able to savor and enjoy the reliving of memories and gain a deeper understanding of who you are and what makes you tick.

There are, of course, many different ways to approach this personal memoir. First of all, it should not, and could not, be done in one day. I think you must go through it at least three times. Many things will be remembered later and added. I promise that when you have it half filled in and can't think of anything more to add, you will soon think of many more things and revisit the entries.

The idea is to list your most cherished memories. A word or phrase is enough. It is not necessary to use detailed explanations, as this is not a diary.

This personal inventory may well help your self-understanding and self-esteem, and it could be a very useful tool in your journey to your highest self.

Finally, remember to note the downside of the "good" and upside of the "bad."

Welcome to your treasure of memories!

The better part
of one's life
consists of his
friendship.

- Abraham Lincoln

BEST FRIENDS

People with whom you share good times and bad,
laughs and tears, throughout the years.
don't forget those with whom you are no longer in touch.

1. __________
2. __________
3. __________
4. __________
5. __________
6. __________
7. __________
8. __________
9. __________
10. __________
11. __________
12. __________
13. __________
14. __________
15. __________
16. __________
17. __________
18. __________
19. __________
20. __________

Those who

bring sunshine

into the lives

of others

cannot keep it

from themselves.

MOST INTERESTING PEOPLE I'VE MET

This can even include people you did not like.

1. ______________________________
2. ______________________________
3. ______________________________
4. ______________________________
5. ______________________________
6. ______________________________
7. ______________________________
8. ______________________________
9. ______________________________
10. ______________________________
11. ______________________________
12. ______________________________
13. ______________________________
14. ______________________________
15. ______________________________
16. ______________________________
17. ______________________________
18. ______________________________
19. ______________________________
20. ______________________________

Hold fast to dreams

for if dreams die,

life is a broken-winged

bird that cannot fly.

- Unknown

HEROES

People who inspired you in one way or another.
heroes comes from all walks of life.
some are in sports, some in education, some in music,
in theater or simply from the neighborhood.

1. ______________________________
2. ______________________________
3. ______________________________
4. ______________________________
5. ______________________________
6. ______________________________
7. ______________________________
8. ______________________________
9. ______________________________
10. ______________________________
11. ______________________________
12. ______________________________
13. ______________________________
14. ______________________________
15. ______________________________
16. ______________________________
17. ______________________________
18. ______________________________
19. ______________________________
20. ______________________________

Humor is my sword

and my shield

It protects me.

You can open a door

with humor and drive

a truck right through.

- Alan Simpson

FUNNIEST STORIES FROM SCHOOL

Ah, youth! Some of the greatest and some of the toughest times in our lives were at school.

1. ______________________________

____

____

____

2. ______________________________

____

____

____

3. ______________________________

____

____

____

4. ______________________________

____

____

____

5. ______________________________

____

____

____

Cherish yesterday...

Dream tomorrow...

Live today.

BEST TIMES

They still make you smile and feel good inside—
The greatest moments and periods of your life.

1. ______________________________
2. ______________________________
3. ______________________________
4. ______________________________
5. ______________________________
6. ______________________________
7. ______________________________
8. ______________________________
9. ______________________________
10. ______________________________
11. ______________________________
12. ______________________________
13. ______________________________
14. ______________________________
15. ______________________________
16. ______________________________
17. ______________________________
18. ______________________________
19. ______________________________
20. ______________________________

FOOTPRINTS

One night a man had a dream.
He dreamed he was walking along
the beach with the LORD. Across the sky
flashed scenes from his life. For each
scene, he noticed two sets of footprints
in the sand: one belonged to him,
and the other to the LORD.

When the last scene of his life flashed
before him, he looked back at the
footprints in the sand. He noticed that
many times along the path of his life
there was only one set of footprints.
He also noticed that it happened at the
very lowest and saddest times in this life.

This really bothered him and he
questioned the LORD about it. "LORD,
you said that once I decided to follow
you, you'd walk with me all the way.
But I have noticed that during the most
troublesome times of my life, there is
only one set of footprints. I don't
understand why, when I needed you
most, you would leave me."

The LORD replied, "My precious,
precious child, I love you and I would
never leave you. During your times
of trial and suffering, when you see only
one set of footprints, it was then that
I carried you."

WORST TIMES

In retrospect, it's interesting. The bad times don't seem as bad...
They don't hurt anymore...Maybe you can even laugh!

1. ______________________________

   ____

2. ______________________________

   ____

3. ______________________________

   ____

4. ______________________________

   ____

5. ______________________________

   ____

6. ______________________________

   ____

7. ______________________________

   ____

8. ______________________________

   ____

9. ______________________________

   ____

10. ______________________________

    ____

Live life

so you never

have to look back

and wish you'd

tried something.

FAVORITE MOVIES

Movies touch us, teach us inspire us, make us laugh and make us cry. What are some of the films that you will never forget? —John Coleman

1. ____________________
2. ____________________
3. ____________________
4. ____________________
5. ____________________
6. ____________________
7. ____________________
8. ____________________
9. ____________________
10. ____________________
11. ____________________
12. ____________________
13. ____________________
14. ____________________
15. ____________________
16. ____________________
17. ____________________
18. ____________________
19. ____________________
20. ____________________

An Irish Tribute

God then Made Man,
The Italian for Music and Art,
The French for Fine Food,
The German for Intelligence,
The Swedes for their Beauty,
The Jew for Religion,
And on and on until
He looked at what
He had created and said,
"This is all very fine, but
No one is having any fun.
I guess I'll have to make me an
IRISHMAN."

FAVORITE TV SHOW

List the most unforgettable episodes and series.
What do you watch today?

1. ____________________
2. ____________________
3. ____________________
4. ____________________
5. ____________________
6. ____________________
7. ____________________
8. ____________________
9. ____________________
10. ____________________
11. ____________________
12. ____________________
13. ____________________
14. ____________________
15. ____________________
16. ____________________
17. ____________________
18. ____________________
19. ____________________
20. ____________________

The only true comment
on a piece of music
is another piece of music.

- Igor Stravinsky

SONGS THAT MEAN SOMETHING TO ME

Music touches times in our lives and chords in our hearts.
It's general and specific. It's wonderful.

1. ______________________________
2. ______________________________
3. ______________________________
4. ______________________________
5. ______________________________
6. ______________________________
7. ______________________________
8. ______________________________
9. ______________________________
10. ______________________________
11. ______________________________
12. ______________________________
13. ______________________________
14. ______________________________
15. ______________________________
16. ______________________________
17. ______________________________
18. ______________________________
19. ______________________________
20. ______________________________

Turn your

stumbling blocks

into stepping stones.

BOOKS

Which are your favorites and why? Is there one you always wanted
To read and are still curious about?
Did one or more dramatically affect your life?

1. ____________________

____

2. ____________________

____

3. ____________________

____

4. ____________________

____

5. ____________________

____

6. ____________________

____

7. ____________________

____

8. ____________________

____

9. ____________________

____

10. ____________________

What hunger is
in relation to food,
zest is in relation
to life.

- Bertrand Russell

FAVORITE FOODS

Include meals, recipes, candy, appetizers, breakfast, lunch, dinner and desserts.

1. ____

2. ____

3. ____

4. ____

5. ____

6. ____

7. ____

8. ____

9. ____

10. ____

Little Things

Most of us
miss out
on life's
big prizes.
The Pulitzer.
The Nobel.
Oscars.
Tonys.
Emmys.
But we're
all eligible
for life's
small pleasures.
A pat
on the back.
A kiss
behind the ear.
A four-pound bass.
A full moon.
An empty
parking space.
A crackling fire.
A great meal.
A glorious sunset.
Hot soup.
Cold beer.
Don't fret
about
copping life's
grand awards.
Enjoy its
tiny delights
There are plenty for all of us.

WATER

Favorite rivers, lakes or oceans.

1. ____

2. ____

3. ____

4. ____

5. ____

6. ____

7. ____

8. ____

9. ____

10. ____

Life

only demands

from you

the strength

you possess.

- Dag Hammarskjőld

MOST EMBARRASSING MOMENTS

Yours, your friends', maybe some you've only heard or read about.

1. ____________________
   ____
2. ____________________
   ____
3. ____________________
   ____
4. ____________________
   ____
5. ____________________
   ____
6. ____________________
   ____
7. ____________________
   ____
8. ____________________
   ____
9. ____________________
   ____
10. ____________________

When I have

listened

to my mistakes

I have grown.

- Hugh Prather

REGRETS

We've all had a few.
Sometimes they weren't so bad...sometimes they were.

1. ____
____
2. ____
____
3. ____
____
4. ____
____
5. ____
____
6. ____
____
7. ____
____
8. ____
____
9. ____
____
10. ____

We all carry it within us:
supreme strength, the fullness
of wisdom, unquenchable joy.
It is never thwarted and cannot
be destroyed.

- Hutsin Smith

LIVING PEOPLE WITH WHOM I'D LIKE TO DINE

...or hang out, party, go to a ball game or a fight, see a movie, watch TV or vacation.

1. ______________________________
2. ______________________________
3. ______________________________
4. ______________________________
5. ______________________________
6. ______________________________
7. ______________________________
8. ______________________________
9. ______________________________
10. ______________________________
11. ______________________________
12. ______________________________
13. ______________________________
14. ______________________________
15. ______________________________
16. ______________________________
17. ______________________________
18. ______________________________
19. ______________________________
20. ______________________________

A true friend

or

a good family

helps your health

as much as

a doctor.

DEAD PEOPLE WITH WHOM I'D LIKE TO DINE

Family, friends, notable historical figures.

1. ______________________________
2. ______________________________
3. ______________________________
4. ______________________________
5. ______________________________
6. ______________________________
7. ______________________________
8. ______________________________
9. ______________________________
10. ______________________________
11. ______________________________
12. ______________________________
13. ______________________________
14. ______________________________
15. ______________________________
16. ______________________________
17. ______________________________
18. ______________________________
19. ______________________________
20. ______________________________

A man's

doubts

and fears

are his worst

enemy.

- William Wrigley, Jr.

BIGGEST FEARS

From snakes to sharks to airplane crashes or fire,
What are yours?

1. ____________________
____
2. ____________________
____
3. ____________________
____
4. ____________________
____
5. ____________________
____
6. ____________________
____
7. ____________________
____
8. ____________________
____
9. ____________________
____
10. ____________________
____

Sin your way

to happiness.

FUNNIEST WORK STORIES

For most, their jobs have elements of drudgery,
But some of the things that would be missed
If we didn't have to go to work are...

1. ______________________________

____

____

____

2. ______________________________

____

____

____

3. ______________________________

____

____

____

4. ______________________________

____

____

____

5. ______________________________

____

____

____

On the outside

one is a star.

But in reality,

one is

completely alone,

doubting everything.

To experience

this loneliness

of soul

is the hardest thing

in the world.

- Brigitte Bardot

IF I COULD CHANGE PLACES WITH SOMEONE, WHO WOULD IT BE AND WHY?

1. ______________________________

____

____

____

2. ______________________________

____

____

____

3. ______________________________

____

____

____

4. ______________________________

____

____

____

5. ______________________________

____

____

____

Attitude is everything.

- John Coleman

INCIDENTS THAT SHAPED MY PERSONALITY

There are incidents in our lives that affect us so much
we are never quite the same.
this may even send us down a different path in life.

1. ______________________________

____

____

____

2. ______________________________

____

____

____

3. ______________________________

____

____

____

4. ______________________________

____

____

____

5. ______________________________

____

____

____

Dreams

come true...

if you make them.

You have to do

the work.

- John Coleman

MY DREAMS

Describe them in a little detail and note both the upside and downside of achieving them.

1.

2.

3.

4.

You have powers you

never dreamed of.

You can do things you

never thought you could do.

There are no limitations

in what you can do except

the limitations in your

own mind as to what

you cannot do.

Don't think you cannot.

Think you can.

- Darwin P. Kingsley

HOW WOULD I LIKE TO BE DIFFERENT?

Your personality, your physical attributes, job status, place in life, health, family situation...

1. ______________________________
____
____
____

2. ______________________________
____
____
____

3. ______________________________
____
____
____

4. ______________________________
____
____
____

5. ______________________________
____
____

The best and

most beautiful

things in the world

cannot be seen

or even touched.

They must be felt

with the heart.

- Helen Keller

DECISIONS THAT CHANGED MY LIFE

What choices altered the path of your life, and why did you make them? How did your life change?

1. ____
____
____
____

2. ____
____
____
____

3. ____
____
____
____

4. ____
____
____
____

5. ____
____
____

Pleasure

is the only thing

to live for.

Nothing ages

like happiness.

- Oscar Wilde

PET PEEVES

What really bugs you—anything and everything!
From personal things to politicians to cats...

1. ____
2. ____
3. ____
4. ____
5. ____
6. ____
7. ____
8. ____
9. ____
10. ____
11. ____
12. ____
13. ____
14. ____
15. ____
16. ____
17. ____
18. ____
19. ____
20. ____

If I accept

the sunshine

and warmth,

I must also accept

the thunder

and the lightning.

- Kahlil Gibran

THINGS I DIDN'T WANT TO DO... BUT I DID

They can change your life.
Did you meet a friend or lover, avoid an accident, bump into a job or career?

1. ____________________

2. ____________________

3. ____________________

4. ____________________

5. ____________________

6. ____________________

7. ____________________

8. ____________________

9. ____________________

10. ____________________

PRESS ON

Nothing in the world can take
the place of persistence.
Talent will not;
Nothing is more common than
Unsuccessful men with talent.
Genius will not;
Unrewarded genius is almost a
proverb.
Education alone will not;
The world is full of educated
derelicts.
Persistence is determination
alone are omnipotent.

BEST TEACHERS

Teaching is the most important profession.
Include coaches and mentors.

1. ____

2. ____

3. ____

4. ____

5. ____

6. ____

7. ____

8. ____

9. ____

10. ____

On Life

What a wonderful life I've had!

I only wish I'd realized it sooner.

- Colette

MENTORS

If you are lucky enough to have had one or more, you are an extremely fortunate person. How did they help?

1. ____
____
____
____

2. ____
____
____
____

3. ____
____
____
____

4. ____
____
____
____

5. ____
____
____
____

In all things of nature
there is something
marvelous.

- Aristotle

BIGGEST INSECURITIES

We all have our own flaws that trouble us.
Sometimes all it takes to accept them is to admit them!

1. ______________________________

____

____

____

2. ______________________________

____

____

____

3. ______________________________

____

____

____

4. ______________________________

____

____

____

5. ______________________________

____

____

____

The poor man

is not he who

is without a cent,

but he who

is without a dream.

- Harry Kemp

FAVORITE PLACES

List the most incredible spots you've ever visited or lived in,
or that have always intrigued you.

1. ______________________________
____
2. ______________________________
____
3. ______________________________
____
4. ______________________________
____
5. ______________________________
____
6. ______________________________
____
7. ______________________________
____
8. ______________________________
____
9. ______________________________
____
10. ______________________________
____

"I love you!"
The three most important
and powerful words
in the world.

- John Coleman

THINGS I WISH I'D SAID

Maybe you were afraid, momentarily speechless
or just wanted to avoid a fight.
Here you can say anything you want without any repercussions.

1. ____

____

____

____

2. ____

____

____

____

3. ____

____

____

____

4. ____

____

____

____

5. ____

____

____

____

It takes a long time

to grow young.

- Pablo Picasso

GUARDIAN ANGELS

If you believe in angels, do you believe they can take human form?
Do angels help us in times of need (and hide their identity)?
When have angels helped you, your friends or your family?

1. ____

2. ____

3. ____

Do not wait for

ideal circumstances,

nor for the best opportunities;

they will never come.

- Janet Erskine Stuart

THANK YOUS

One last chance to say it.
Include the ones left unsaid!

1. ______________________________

____

2. ______________________________

____

3. ______________________________

____

4. ______________________________

____

5. ______________________________

____

6. ______________________________

____

7. ______________________________

____

8. ______________________________

____

9. ______________________________

____

10. ______________________________

____

Love

There is no difficulty that
enough love will not conquer;
No disease that enough love
will not heal;
No door that enough love
will not open;
No gulf that enough love
will not bridge;
No wall that enough love
will not throw down;
No sin that enough love
will not redeem...

It makes no difference how
deeply seated may be the trouble;
How hopeless the outlook;
How muddled the tangle;
How great the mistake.
A sufficient realization of love
will dissolve it all...
If only you could love enough
you would be the happiest and
most powerful being in the world.

- Emmet Fox

IF I HAD KNOWN THEN…

…what I know now.
things you would have done differently,
but you didn't know better at the time…

1. ______________________________

____

2. ______________________________

____

3. ______________________________

____

4. ______________________________

____

5. ______________________________

____

6. ______________________________

____

7. ______________________________

____

8. ______________________________

____

9. ______________________________

____

10. ______________________________

____

Three things in human life
are important.
The first is to be kind.
The second is to be kind.
The third is to be kind.

- Henry James

GOOD DEEDS

The ways you've helped others.
Be proud of yourself and do some more.

1. ______________________________
____
2. ______________________________
____
3. ______________________________
____
4. ______________________________
____
5. ______________________________
____
6. ______________________________
____
7. ______________________________
____
8. ______________________________
____
9. ______________________________
____
10. ______________________________
____

To the person with a toothache,
even if the world is tottering,
there is nothing more important
than a visit to the dentist.

- George Bernard Shaw

BEST FEATURES

Physical and other.

1. ____________________

2. ____________________

3. ____________________

4. ____________________

5. ____________________

There are no victims

—only volunteers.

- Billi Gordon

BIGGEST FAULTS

We all have them. What are yours?

1. ____
____
____
____

2. ____
____
____
____

3. ____
____
____
____

4. ____
____
____
____

5. ____
____
____
____

I'm tired of

all this nonsense

about beauty being

only skin deep.

That's deep enough.

What do you want—

and adorable pancreas?

- Jean Kerr

PHYSICAL FLAWS

Did you know that everyone else has them, too?
Some people don't like their own hair. Many don't like their height.
You don't like...

1. ______________________________
____
____
____

2. ______________________________
____
____
____

3. ______________________________
____
____
____

4. ______________________________
____
____
____

5. ______________________________
____
____
____

Passion—

There simply

can be nothing more.

There simply

should be nothing less.

- Jeanne (Jhett) Jensen

THINGS TO DO

List your top 20.

1. ______________________________
2. ______________________________
3. ______________________________
4. ______________________________
5. ______________________________
6. ______________________________
7. ______________________________
8. ______________________________
9. ______________________________
10. ______________________________
11. ______________________________
12. ______________________________
13. ______________________________
14. ______________________________
15. ______________________________
16. ______________________________
17. ______________________________
18. ______________________________
19. ______________________________
20. ______________________________

Take time to work—
it is the price of success.
Take time to think—
it is the source of power.
Take time to play—
it is the secret to perpetual youth.
Take time to read—
it is the foundation of wisdom.
Take time to be friendly—
it is the road to happiness.
Take time to dream—
it is hitching your wagon to a star.
Take time to love and be loved—
it is the privilege of the Gods.
Take time to look around—
the day is too short to be selfish.
Take time to laugh—
It is the music of the soul.

- An Old Irish Prayer

TEN TIMES I'VE CRIED

Movies, onions, frustrations, childhood bumps...
and other big hurts or sadnesses.

1. ______________________________
____
2. ______________________________
____
3. ______________________________
____
4. ______________________________
____
5. ______________________________
____
6. ______________________________
____
7. ______________________________
____
8. ______________________________
____
9. ______________________________
____
10. ______________________________
____

A graceful and

honorable old age

is the childhood

of immortality.

- Pindar

WHAT'S KEEPING ME FROM ACHIEVING WHAT I WANT?

1. ____
____
____
____

2. ____
____
____
____

3. ____
____
____
____

4. ____
____
____
____

5. ____
____
____
____

A light heart lives long.

- William Shakespeare

PLEDGES TO MYSELF

Many people want to lose weight but few keep it off.
Before my life is over, I promise to...

1. ____

2. ____

3. ____

4. ____

5. ____

Perfection does not exist.
To understand this
is the triumph
of human intelligence;
to expect to possess it
is the most dangerous
kind of madness.

- Alfred de Raisset

FAVORITE VACATIONS

Where? When? With Whom?
What's your favorite memory?

1. ______________________________
____

2. ______________________________
____

3. ______________________________
____

4. ______________________________
____

5. ______________________________
____

6. ______________________________
____

7. ______________________________
____

8. ______________________________
____

9. ______________________________
____

10. ______________________________
____

It is a very funny thing
about life:
if you refuse to accept
anything but the best
you very often get it.

- W. Somerset Maugham

TRIPS TO TAKE

Where? Why? With whom? When?

1. ____

2. ____

3. ____

4. ____

5. ____

6. ____

7. ____

8. ____

9. ____

10. ____

I will make

this day

a happy one,

for I alone

can determine

what kind of day

it will be.

BEST PRACTICAL JOKES

That you played, were played on you or you witnessed at your school, work or in your neighborhood.

1. ______________________________
____
2. ______________________________
____
3. ______________________________
____
4. ______________________________
____
5. ______________________________
____
6. ______________________________
____
7. ______________________________
____
8. ______________________________
____
9. ______________________________
____
10. ______________________________
____

Do not stand at my grave and weep,

I am not there, I do not sleep

I am a thousand winds that blow,

I am the diamond glints on snow.

I am the sunlight on ripened grain;

I am the gentle autumn's rain.

When you awaken in the morning's hush,

I am the swift uplifting rush

Of quiet birds in circled flight

I am the soft star that shines at night.

Do not stand at my grave and cry.

I am not there; I did not die.

- Unknown

ONE YEAR TILL PAINLESS DEATH

If death was painless, and you knew it would be peaceful, would you still fear it? What would you say, do, feel in the meantime?

1. ____
____
2. ____
____
3. ____
____
4. ____
____
5. ____
____
6. ____
____
7. ____
____
8. ____
____
9. ____
____
10. ____
____

The secret

of staying young

is to live honestly,

eat slowly,

and lie about

your age.

- Lucille Ball

THREE WISHES

If you had Aladdin's lamp, what would they be?
Rub away...

1. ______________________________

2. ______________________________

3. ______________________________

It's pretty hard

to tell what does

bring happiness;

poverty and wealth

have both failed.

- Kim Hubbard

MONEY

What victories and defeats have you known in the game of money?

1. ______________________________

____

____

____

2. ______________________________

____

____

____

3. ______________________________

____

____

____

4. ______________________________

____

____

____

5. ______________________________

____

____

____

No girl, however

intelligent and warmhearted,

can possibly know or feel

half as much at 20

as she will at 35.

- Stephen Vizinczey

ADVENTURES

What are the wildest things you ever did?
What are the craziest things you want to do?

1. ______________________________
   ____
2. ______________________________
   ____
3. ______________________________
   ____
4. ______________________________
   ____
5. ______________________________
   ____
6. ______________________________
   ____
7. ______________________________
   ____
8. ______________________________
   ____
9. ______________________________
   ____
10. ______________________________
    ____

If you can dream it

you can do it.

- Bud Greenspan

PERSONAL ACCOMPLISHMENTS

Your proudest moments and best deeds.
Even if they seemed small at the time, how did they help?

1. ____

2. ____

3. ____

4. ____

5. ____

If we'd only stop trying

to be happy, we'd have

a pretty good time.

- Edith Wharton

BIGGEST LESSONS LEARNED

The most important truths you have come to know in your lifetime.

1. ______________________________

____

2. ______________________________

____

3. ______________________________

____

4. ______________________________

____

5. ______________________________

____

6. ______________________________

____

7. ______________________________

____

8. ______________________________

____

9. ______________________________

____

10. ______________________________

____

Unless each day
can be looked back upon
by an individual as one
in which he has some fun,
some joy, some real
satisfaction,
That day is a loss.

- Dwight D. Eisenhower

CONCERTS, PLAYS, PERFORMANCES

Live events can be incredibly thrilling and remembered for a lifetime.

1. ______________________________

   ____

2. ______________________________

   ____

3. ______________________________

   ____

4. ______________________________

   ____

5. ______________________________

   ____

6. ______________________________

   ____

7. ______________________________

   ____

8. ______________________________

   ____

9. ______________________________

   ____

10. ______________________________

Enjoy the little things,

For one day you may

Look back and realize

They were the big things.

- Robert Brault

FAVORITE PETS

Animals often become a treasured family member and enrich our lives.

1. ____

____

____

____

2. ____

____

____

____

3. ____

____

____

____

4. ____

____

____

____

5. ____

____

____

____

Forgive all who

have offended you,

not for them,

but for yourself.

- Harriet Utz Nelson

BIGGEST FIGHTS AND QUARRELS

Our relationships can be heart-wrenching or funny. We may want to forget the rancorous times but sometimes we carry them around for too long. Get them out of the way.

1. ______________________________

____

____

____

2. ______________________________

____

____

____

3. ______________________________

____

____

____

4. ______________________________

____

____

____

5. ______________________________

____

____

____

If you want others

to be happy,

practice compassion.

if you want to be happy,

practice compassion.

- Unknown

MEMORABLE NEIGHBORS

They can either make life easier and more enjoyable.
Or they can make it rougher and be a huge problem.

1. ____

2. ____

3. ____

4. ____

5. ____

Happiness is to be found

along the way,

not at the end of the road,

for then the journey

is over and it is too late.

- Robert R. Updegraff

PARTIES AND CELEBRATIONS

Times spent celebrating with others are often the most anticipated and fun occasions in our lives.

1. ____
2.
3.
4.
5.
6.
7.
8.
9.
10.

If you survive long

enough, you're

revered—rather like

an old building.

- Katherine Hepburn

MOST MEMORABLE PROJECTS

As a child or an adult; in school or at work—
what have been your most memorable hobbies or undertakings?

1. ____
____
2. ____
____
3. ____
____
4. ____
____
5. ____
____
6. ____
____
7. ____
____
8. ____
____
9. ____
____
10. ____
____

Get action.

Do things; don't fritter

away your time.

Take a place wherever

you are and

be somebody.

- Theodore Roosevelt

FAVORITE JOBS

We've all probably held more than a few. Which ones did you love And which ones did you loathe?

1. ______________________________

____

____

____

2. ______________________________

____

____

____

3. ______________________________

____

____

____

4. ______________________________

____

____

____

5. ______________________________

____

____

____

To forgive is the highest,
most beautiful form
of love. In return you
will receive untold peace
and happiness.

- Robert Muller

MOST INFURIATING PEOPLE

Some people are so irritating that they leave you speechless.
Who pushed your buttons?

1. ______________________________

____

2. ______________________________

____

3. ______________________________

____

4. ______________________________

____

5. ______________________________

____

6. ______________________________

____

7. ______________________________

____

8. ______________________________

____

9. ______________________________

____

10. ______________________________

____

More than enough

is too much.

- Unknown

HOLIDAYS

Too much partying, too much family, but moments you will never forget.

1.

2.

3.

4.

5.

Unhappy is the man
whom man can
make unhappy.

- Ralph Waldo Emerson

FAVORITE (AND NOT-SO-FAVORITE) SPORTS HEROES

Who were the ones you rooted for and who were the ones you hated?

1. ______________________________
____
2. ______________________________
____
3. ______________________________
____
4. ______________________________
____
5. ______________________________
____
6. ______________________________
____
7. ______________________________
____
8. ______________________________
____
9. ______________________________
____
10. ______________________________
____

There are risks and costs
to a program of action,
but they are less
than the long-range risks
and costs of comfortable
inaction.

- *John F. Kennedy*

TIME CAPSULE

If you could put things away for future generations, what would they be and why?

1. ______________________________
____
2. ______________________________
____
3. ______________________________
____
4. ______________________________
____
5. ______________________________
____
6. ______________________________
____
7. ______________________________
____
8. ______________________________
____
9. ______________________________
____
10. ______________________________
____

When I was about eight,
I decided that the most
wonderful thing,
next to a human being,
was a book.

- Margaret Walker

WRITERS

Poets, songwriters, newspaper columnists, and authors.
Who taught you a new way to look at things or simply captured your heart?

1. ______________________________
____
2. ______________________________
____
3. ______________________________
____
4. ______________________________
____
5. ______________________________
____
6. ______________________________
____
7. ______________________________
____
8. ______________________________
____
9. ______________________________
____
10. ______________________________
____

In search of my

mother's garden

I found my own.

- Alice Walker

FLOWERS, PLANTS AND TREES

The simple and often majestic qualities of these wonderful creations: the beauty of the gladiola, the essence of jasmine, and the shade of the elm.

1. ____________________
2. ____________________
3. ____________________
4. ____________________
5. ____________________
6. ____________________
7. ____________________
8. ____________________
9. ____________________
10. ____________________

My favorite thing is to go

where I've never been.

- Diane Arbus

SECRET PLACES

Where have you gone for solitude, peace and quiet?

1. ____

2. ____

3. ____

4. ____

5. ____

Only the upright heart

that has its own logic and

its own reason is free.

- Marc Chagall

ADVICE

What are some of the most rewarding words of encouragement you have heard? Who said them?

1. ____

2. ____

3. ____

4. ____

5. ____

The great thing about
getting older is that you
don't lose all the other
ages you've been.

- Madeleine L'Engle

GAMES

What are the games you loved as a child?
Which ones do you play now?

1. ______________________________

____

____

____

____

____

2. ______________________________

____

____

____

____

____

3. ______________________________

____

____

____

____

____

Being independent,

answering to no one

and doing whatever

you want is one

of the two greatest

things in life.

The greatest is

sharing love.

- John Coleman

DARKEST HOURS

What were the lowest times of your life and how did you get through them?

1. ____

2. ____

3. ____

4. ____

5. ____

A sense of humor

can help you

overlook

the unattractive,

tolerate

the unpleasant,

cope with

the unexpected,

and smile

through

the unbearable.

- Moshe Waldoks

FAVORITE JOKES

It is said that "laughter is the best medicine."
So what are the jokes that made you laugh?

1. ____________________

____

____

____

2. ____________________

____

____

____

3. ____________________

____

____

____

4. ____________________

____

____

____

5. ____________________

____

____

____

I have no regrets.

I wouldn't have lived

my life the way

I did if I was going

to worry about

what people were

going to say.

- Ingrid Bergman

WHAT DO YOU BELIEVE ABOUT SPIRITUALITY, GOD AND LIFE AFTER DEATH?

1. ______________________________

2. ______________________________

3. ______________________________

4. ______________________________

5. ______________________________

On Laughter.

He who laughs, lasts.

- Mary Pettibone Poole

BIGGEST CHANGES IN THE WORLD IN YOUR LIFETIME

1. ____

____

____

____

2. ____

____

____

____

3. ____

____

____

____

4. ____

____

____

____

5. ____

____

____

____

I wish it were OK

in this country to look

one's age, whatever it is.

Maturity has a lot going for it,

even in terms of aesthetics.

For example, you no longer

get bubblegum stuck

in your braces.

- Cyra McFadden

FAVORITE ARTWORK

Any image you treasure (even your own or your childrens'!)...

1.

2.

3.

4.

5.

Tell me what

you eat

and I will tell you

what you are.

- Anthelme Brillat-Savarin

FAVORITE PHOTOS OF MYSELF

Admit it. No false modesty. Paste them below.

Never fear

that your life

might come

to an end;

Rather, fear

that it should

never begin.

FUNERAL PLAN

How would you like to be remembered?
If your funeral went exactly as you wished, how would it be?
Don't be afraid to use humor—jokes, remembrances, testimonials—
and break traditions. Who would speak?

1. ______________________________

____

____

____

2. ______________________________

____

____

____

3. ______________________________

____

____

____

4. ______________________________

____

____

____

5. ______________________________

____

____

____

Let me observe,

with new interest,

even the commonplace

things that happen

in each new day.

- Unknown

PRIZED POSSESSIONS

Favorite souvenirs, mementos and items that have a priceless value in your heart.

1. ______________________________
____
2. ______________________________
____
3. ______________________________
____
4. ______________________________
____
5. ______________________________
____
6. ______________________________
____
7. ______________________________
____
8. ______________________________
____
9. ______________________________
____
10. ______________________________
____

FAMILY TREE

Everyone's family is different,
so feel free to define your own family
by adding whatever branches you need.

GREAT GRANDMOTHER GREAT GRANDFATHER
GREAT GRANDMOTHER GREAT GRANDFATHER

GRANDMOTHER GRANDFATHER

FATHER

ME

GREAT GRANDMOTHER GREAT GRANDFATHER
GREAT GRANDMOTHER GREAT GRANDFATHER

GRANDMOTHER GRANDFATHER

MOTHER

ME

NOTES

NOTES